Giftbooks in this series by Helen Exley:

Words on Hope
Words on Courage
Words of Wisdom

Words on Joy
Words on Kindness
Words on Love and Caring

Published simultaneously in 1997 by Exley Publications in
Great Britain, and Exley Giftbooks in the USA.
Copyright © Helen Exley 1998
The moral right of the author has been asserted.

12 11 10 9 8 7 6 5 4 3 2

Edited and pictures selected by Helen Exley
ISBN 1-85015-920-3

Picture research by Image Select International.
Typeset by Delta, Watford.
Printed in China.

**Exley Publications Ltd, 16 Chalk Hill, Watford,
Herts WD1 4BN, UK.
Exley Publications LLC, 232 Madison Avenue,
Suite 1206, NY 10016, USA.**

Words on Courage

A HELEN EXLEY
GIFTBOOK

EXLEY
NEW YORK • WATFORD, UK

Courage is, with love,
the greatest gift.
We are, each of us, defeated
many times — but if we accept
defeat with cheerfulness,
and learn from it,
and try another way —
then we will find
fulfilment.

ROSANNE AMBROSE-BROWN

The glory
is not in never failing,
but in rising every time
you fall.

CHINESE PROVERB

Where is the university
for courage?... The university
for courage is to do
what you believe in!

EL CORDOBES,

Shrug off the restraints
that you have allowed
others to place upon you.
You are limitless.
There is nothing you cannot
achieve.
There is no sadness in life
That cannot be reversed....

CLEARWATER

I have a lot of things
to prove to myself.
One is that I can live
my life fearlessly.

OPRAH WINFREY
b 1954

I am
only one;
but still
I am one.
I cannot
do everything,
but still
I can do
something;
I will not
refuse to
do something
I can do.

HELEN KELLER
(1880-1968)

The baby rises to its feet,
takes a step,
is overcome with triumph
and joy —
and falls flat on its face.
It is a pattern for all that is
to come!
But learn from the bewildered
baby. Lurch to your feet again.
You'll make the sofa
in the end.

PAM BROWN
b 1928

Feel the fear, and do it
anyway.

SUSAN JEFFERS

Don't be afraid to take big steps.
You can't cross a chasm
in two small jumps.

DAVID LLOYD GEORGE (1863-1945)

What matters is not the size
of the dog in the fight, but
the size of the fight in the dog.

COACH BEAR BRYANT

Life is either a daring adventure or nothing. To keep our faces toward change and behave like free spirits in the presence of fate is strength undefeatable.

HELEN KELLER (1880-1968)

I wanted you to see what real courage is, instead of getting the idea that courage is a man with a gun in his hand.
It's when you know you're licked before you begin but you begin anyway and you see it through no matter what.

HARPER LEE

Courage is
resistance to
fear, mastery
of fear, not
absence of fear.

MARK TWAIN
(1835-1910)

How can you hesitate? Risk!
Risk anything!
Care no more for the opinion
of others, for those voices.
Do the hardest thing on earth
for your. Act for yourself.
Face the truth.

KATHERINE MANSFIELD
(1888-1923)

WHEN YOUR BOW IS BROKEN

AND YOUR LAST ARROW SPENT,

THEN SHOOT, SHOOT

WITH YOUR WHOLE HEART.

ZEN SAYING

WHEN YOU GET INTO
A TIGHT PLACE AND EVERYTHING
GOES AGAINST YOU,
TILL IT SEEMS AS THOUGH
YOU COULD NOT HANG ON
A MINUTE LONGER,
NEVER GIVE UP THEN,
FOR THAT IS JUST THE PLACE
AND TIME
THAT THE TIDE WILL TURN.

HARRIET BEECHER STOWE
(1811-1896)

You gain strength, courage,
and confidence by every
experience in which you really
stop to look fear in the face.
You are able to say to yourself,
"I lived through this horror.
I can take the next thing
that comes along."...
You must do the thing you
think you cannot do.

ELEANOR ROOSEVELT
(1884-1962)

The only courage that matters is the kind that gets you from one moment to the next.

MIGNON MCLAUGHLIN

It isn't for
the moment
you are struck
that you need.
courage,
but for
the long
uphill climb
back to
sanity
and faith
and security.

ANNE MORROW
LINDBERGH
b 1906

E.Longoni

To those of us whose lives
have been hidden from society,
from those we love, from ourselves,
we join in solidarity.
To those of us who have resisted
isolation and stood up to fear,
we give heartfelt affirmation.
In honor of those of us who have
courageously, joyfully, burst into
the fullness of our identities,
we offer gratitude and blessing.

MOLLY FUMIA

"*Zidele amathambo.*"
Give yourself up,
bones as well.
(i.e. take a chance!)

SOUTH AFRICAN
NDEBELE SAYING

The man with courage
is a majority

ANDREW JACKSON

If our people are to fight
their way up out of bondage
we must arm them
with the sword and the shield
and the buckler of pride — belief in
themselves and their possibilities,
based upon a sure knowledge of
the achievements of the past.

MARY MCLEOD BETHUNE

"This too will pass."
I was taught these words by
my grandmother as a phrase
that is to be used at _all_ times
in your life. When things are
spectacularly dreadful; when things are
absolutely appalling; when everything is
superb and wonderful and marvellous
and happy
say these four words to yourself.
They will give you a sense of perspective
and help you also
to make the most of what is
good and be stoical about
what is bad.

CLAIRE RAYNER

There is no handicap so great
in life as the lack of courage
to go on after loss or failure.

PAM BROWN
b.1928

IF YOU HAVE MADE MISTAKES...
THERE IS ALWAYS ANOTHER
CHANCE FOR YOU... YOU MAY
HAVE A FRESH START ANY
MOMENT YOU CHOOSE, FOR THIS
THING WE CALL "FAILURE" IS
NOT THE FALLING DOWN,
BUT THE STAYING DOWN.

MARY PICKFORD
(1893-1979)

They blaze through history –
the heros and the heroines.
Those who stood alone against
great odds. Those who endured
intolerable suffering rather than

betray companions. Those who
ignored danger to save others.
Sudden unpremeditated acts —
or a long perseverance.
The world is built upon the courage
of a million million unremembered
souls, whose courage has outlived
pestilence and war, bereavement,
failure, suffering of every kind —
and given life and hope to all
who followed them.

PAM BROWN,
b. 1928

Give us grace, O God, to dare
to do the deed which we well
know cries to be done.
Let us not hesitate because of ease,
or the words of [people's] mouths,
or our own lives. Mighty causes
are calling us — the freeing of
women, the training of children
the putting down of hate and
murder and poverty — all these
and more. But they call with
voices that mean work
and sacrifice and death.
[May we find a way to meet
the task.]

W. E. B. DU BOIS

What will see me through
the next 20 years
(and I am less sure of those 20
than I was of "forever") is my
knowledge that even in the face
of the sweeping away of all
that I assumed to be permanent,
even when the universe made it
quite clear to me that I was
mistaken in my certainties,
in my definitions, I did not break.
The shattering of my sureties
did not shatter me.
Stability comes from inside,
not outside....

LUCILLE CLIFTON

THE COURAGE OF VERY ORDINARY
PEOPLE IS ALL THAT STANDS
BETWEEN US AND THE DARK.

PAM BROWN,
b 1928

Disasters sweep the world —
war and disease, earthquake
and flood and fire — but always
in their wake come acts
of courage and concern that
astound the human heart.
Light in utter darkness.

CHARLOTTE GRAY,
b 1937

ONLY ONE PRINCIPLE WILL GIVE
YOU COURAGE, THAT IS THE
PRINCIPLE THAT NO EVIL LASTS
FOR EVER NOR INDEED FOR
VERY LONG.

EPICURUS (341-271 B.C.)

There is the courage that springs
from battle fever, or from
a desperate emergency.
And there is a courage that is
rooted in the acceptance
of a dreadful circumstance,
and all that it entails —
a courage that brings sanity
and cheerfulness and hope
to lives that could be utterly
consumed by sorrow.
This is the courage that endures.
This is the greatest bravery.

PAM BROWN
b . 1928

To endure is greater than to dare;
to tire out hostile fortune;
to be daunted by no difficulty;
to keep heart when all have lost it —
who can say this is not greatness?

WILLIAM MAKEPEACE THACKERAY
(1811-1863)

Courage looks you straight in the eye. She is not impressed with power trippers, and she knows first aid. Courage is not afraid to weep, and she is not afraid to pray, even when she is not sure who she is praying to.

When she walks it is clear
she has made the journey from
loneliness to solitude.
The people who told me
she was stern were not lying;
they just forgot to mention
she was kind.

J. RUTH GENDLER

If I were asked to give what
I consider the single most useful
bit of advice for all humanity,
it would be this: Expect trouble as
an inevitable part of life,
and when it comes, hold your head
high, look it squarely in the eye
and say, "I will be bigger than you.
You cannot defeat me."
Then repeat to yourself the most
comforting of all words,
"This too shall pass."

ANN LANDERS

We ought to remember
that we are not the only ones
to find ourselves at an
apparent impasse.
Just as a kite rises
against the wind, even the
worst of troubles can
strengthen us.
As thousands before us
have met the identical fate
and mastered it, so can we!

DR. R. BRASCH

*All serious daring
starts from within.*

EUDORA WELTY

... victory is often a thing deferred, and rarely at the summit of courage.... What is at the summit of courage, I think, is freedom. The freedom that comes with the knowledge that no earthly power can break you; that an unbroken spirit is the only thing you cannot live without; that in the end it is the courage of conviction that moves things, that makes all change possible.

PAULA GIDDINGS

Empower me
to be a bold participant,
rather than a timid saint in waiting,
in the difficult ordinariness of now;
to exercise the authority of honesty,
rather than to defer to power,
or deceive to get it,
to influence someone for justice,
rather than impress anyone for gain;
and, by grace, to find treasures
of joy, or friendship, of peace
hidden in the fields of the daily
you give me to plow.

TED LODER

The ideals which have lighted my way, and time after time have given me new courage

to face life cheerfully, have been
kindness, beauty, and truth....

ALBERT EINSTEIN
(1879-1955)

Courage takes many forms.
There is physical courage, there is
moral courage. Then there is a still
higher type of courage —
the courage to brave pain, to live
with it, to never let others know
of it and to still find joy in life;
to wake up in the morning with
an enthusiasm for the day ahead.

HOWARD COSELL

Hold on;
HOLD FAST;
HOLD OUT.
PATIENCE IS GENIUS.

COMTE DÉ BUFFON

Our way is not soft grass,
it's a mountain path
with lots of rocks.
But it goes upwards,
forward, toward
the sun.

RUTH WESTHEIMER

STORMS MAKE OAKS

TAKE DEEPER ROOT.

GEORGE HERBERT
(1593-1633)

We see her pass, her furry hat at a jaunty angle on her auburn curls, her face cheerful with paint and powder – and meet her smiles with smiles. For she is younger than us all, though she is ninety-three – relishing the sunlight, the promises of spring. Old and frail and sick and relishing the day.

Concerned for all about her. "Me? I get along! You have to, don't you, Dear?"

Carrying her courage lightly in the sun. Her sorrows hidden in her heart.

PAM BROWN, b. 1928

Tho' much is taken, much abides; and tho'
We are not now that strength which in old days
Moved earth and heaven; that which we are, we are;
One equal temper of heroic hearts,
Made weak by time and fate, but strong in will
To strive, to seek, to find, and not to yield.

ALFRED, LORD TENNYSON
(1809-1892)

I have accepted fear as a part of life – specifically the fear of change.... I have gone ahead despite the pounding in the heart that says: turn back.

ERICA JONG, b. 1942

HOLD YOUR HEAD HIGH, STICK YOUR CHEST OUT. YOU CAN MAKE IT. IT GETS DARK SOMETIMES BUT MORNING COMES.... KEEP HOPE ALIVE.

JESSE JACKSON, b. 1941

You can transcend all negativity
when you realize that the only
power it has over you
is your belief in it.
As you experience this truth
about yourself you are
set free.

EILEEN CADDY

I was always looking outside
myself for strength
and confidence but it comes
from within.
It is there all the time.

ANNA FREUD (1895-1982)

Acknowledgements: The publishers are grateful for permission to reproduce copyright material. Whilst every effort has been made to trace copyright holders, the publishers would be pleased to hear from any not here acknowledged. MOLLY FUMIA: From *A Safe Passage* by Molly Fumia, copyright © 1992 Molly Fumia published by Conari Press. TED LODER: Excerpt from *Wrestling the Light: Ache and Awe in the Human-Divine Struggle* by Ted Loder, copyright © 1991 Innisfree Press, reprinted by permission of Innisfree Press, Philadelphia, Pennsylvania, USA. PIED RICHE: Reprinted with permission of Council Oak Books from *A Cherokee Feast of Days* by Joyce Sequichie Hifler: copyright © 1992 by Joyce Sequichie Hifler.

Picture Credits: Exley Publications would like to thank the following organizations and individuals for permission to reproduce their pictures. Whilst every effort has been made to trace copyright holders, the publishers would be pleased to hear from any not here acknowledged. AISA, Alinari, Archiv Für Kunst (AKG), Bridgeman Art Library (BAL), Christie's Images, Edimedia (EDM), Superstock (SS).Cover and title page: © 1997 Fernando C. Amorsolo, *Pacific Waves;* page 7: Gorot, Villa D'Arvray, AISA; page 8: Pierre Prins, *Sunset*, EDM; page 10: A. Gallen Kalella, *The river Imatra in winter*, AISA; page 12/13: © 1997 Amado A. Hidalso, *Serenity 1992;* page 14: Paul Cèzanne, *Turn in the road;* page 16: © 1997 Diosdado Lorenzo, *Peasant Girl;* page 18: Jean Baptiste Camille